the little book of
UNITY

Hardie Grant

QUADRILLE

Unity

Definition:
noun

The state of being united, or joined as a whole.

Do not confuse unity with uniformity.

"It is not in numbers, but in unity, that our great strength lies."

THOMAS PAINE

Unity: a word, an idea, an activity that brims with warmth and connection.

Synonyms

- Agreement
- Concord
- Consensus
- Harmony
- Interconnection
- Oneness
- Solidarity
- Totality

Unity comes from the Latin root *uni*, meaning 'one'. Other words from the same root include:

- Unison, meaning 'one sound'
- Unified, meaning 'made into one'
- Unanimous, meaning 'of one mind'
- Unique, meaning 'only'
- Unilateral, meaning 'one-sided'
- Unicorn, meaning 'one horn'

"Those who know do not speak;
Those who speak do not know.
Stop up the openings,
Close down the doors,
Rub off the sharp edges.
Unravel all confusion.
Harmonize the light,
Give up contention:
This is called finding the unity of life."

LAO TSU

*"We cannot live only for ourselves.
A thousand fibres connect us with
our fellow men."*

HENRY MELVILL

Unity is saying. . .

"Please join us."

"Come in."

"All are welcome here."

"Make yourself at home."

"We're different. . . Let's learn from each other."

Foster unity by offering a warm welcome to anyone who needs it

Instead of waiting for others to make the first move, reach out and connect with people in your community. Whether it's picking up some groceries for an elderly neighbour, baking a cake for the people who've just moved to the area or just saying a simple hello, you can make a huge difference to the people around you.

Chemistry teaches us that unity is essential to life on earth. That most famous of chemical compounds, H_2O, is a fusion of separate entities, hydrogen and oxygen. They are two separate entities, but when united together create one invaluable substance: water.

Remember that you are a wonderful unique creature formed of a multitude of cells – approximately 15 trillion – with even more non-human microbes. As such an extraordinary biological creature, consider that your entire body moves in constant unity.

Every movement you make, every feeling you experience, every change in temperature, blood sugar and blood pressure is caused by interactions between your cells. You are a whole unique ecosystem.

When you next feel disunity between your mind and body, think of the ecosystem that exists inside you

Remember: you are an organism that is constantly working in flux and unity, even when you don't feel it. Pause, breathe deeply and wait for equilibrium to return.

"A sound mind in a sound body is a short but full description of a happy state in this world; he that has these two has little more to wish for."

JOHN LOCKE

Discover the unity inherent in yoga

The word yoga is derived from the Sanskrit root yuj, meaning 'to join' or 'to unite'. Yoga aims to forge a union between body, mind and spirit, as well as between the individual self and universal consciousness.

The meaning of *namasté*

My soul honours your soul.
I honour the place in you
Where the entire universe resides.

I honour the light, love, truth,
Beauty and peace within you,
Because it is also within me.

In sharing these things
We are united, we are the same,
We are one.

*"The lamps are different,
but the Light is the same."*

RUMI

"Until we realize the unity of life, we live in fear."

Upanishads

The blind men and the elephant

An ancient story first recorded in the Buddhist scripture *Udana* tells of a king who invites six blind men to describe an elephant.

He who felt the tusk said, 'The elephant, Your Majesty, is just like the pole of a plough.' The blind man who touched the ear said, 'The elephant, Your Majesty, is just like a winnowing basket.' He who described the tuft at the end of the tail said, 'The elephant, Your Majesty, is just like a broom.' Not one of the men was able to describe the whole magnificent beast.

In some versions of the story, the blind men all come to blows, disagreeing violently about what they have each felt. In others, they piece together their separate experiences and eventually 'see' the shape of the elephant.

Some interpretations view the elephant as God and the blind men as religions all squabbling over their own idea of the Almighty. Others use the story to illustrate that human tendency to focus solely on our own experiences – and to show that we should take the time to learn from others.

When problem solving, remember the Blind Men and the Elephant

The next time you are with your family, friends or work colleagues attempting to tackle a problem, be conscious of the limits of your own experience. Make sure you share your thoughts and experiences – and listen to others' – to face the problem with a rounded perspective.

"So powerful is the light of unity that it can illuminate the whole earth."

BAHÁ'U'LLÁH

"From out of all the many particulars comes oneness, and out of oneness come all the many particulars."

HERACLITUS

"Do not follow the ideas of others, but learn to listen to the voice within yourself. Your body and mind will become clear and you will realize the unity of all things."

DOGEN

"The great lesson is, that unity is behind all. Call it God, Love, Spirit. Allah, Jehovah – it is the same unity that animates all life from the lowest animal to the noblest man."

SWAMI VIVEKANANDA

"Everything above and below is one unity."

BAAL SHEM TOV

"In reality all are members of one human family – children of one Heavenly Father. Humanity may be likened unto the vari-coloured flowers of one garden. There is unity in diversity. Each sets off and enhances the other's beauty."

'ABDU'L-BAHÁ

"He who experiences the unity of life sees his own Self in all beings, and all beings in his own Self."

Bhagavad Gita

"Above all, clothe yourselves with love, which binds us all together in perfect harmony."

Colossians 3:14

"*Let what seems a barrier become a path, and let us unite, not in spite of our differences, but through them. For differences can never be wiped away, and life would be so much the poorer without them. Let all human races keep their own personalities, and yet come together, not in a uniformity that is dead, but in a unity that is living.*"

RABINDRANATH TAGORE

The Bulls and the Lion

There once was a hungry lion who saw a field with three bulls. As they ate the sweet grass of the field together, the lion approached; the bulls fought off the lion with their horns, and the lion knew he could not catch them together. So, he whispered lies and gossip to sow the seeds of distrust. The lion crept to the edge of the field and watched the bulls leave each other and each stand alone eating grass in different corners of the field. Then he pounced and ate the bulls one by one.

'The Bulls and the Lion' is one of Aesop's fables, which carries the message that in unity is strength. The fable also reminds us to trust our friends – and perhaps to seek the whole story before we react.

Heraclitus, a philosopher who lived around 500 BC, put forward the theory of the Unity of Opposites. He sought to show that opposites are interconnected and that all things are made up of unified but contradictory parts.

Take inspiration from Heraclitus and remember: unity does not mean sameness.

" *Collections: wholes and not wholes; brought together, pulled apart; sung in unison, sung in conflict; from all things one and from one all things.*"

HERACLITUS

"Do I contradict myself?
Very well then I contradict myself,
(I am large, I contain multitudes.)"

WALT WHITMAN

"Love is the cause of unity in all things."

ARISTOTLE

René Descartes, a 16th century French philosopher, examined the duality of mind and body. In his *Meditations* he declared that the soul and body are not two separate entities but are bound together inextricably.

"Nature also teaches me, by these sensations of pain, hunger, thirst and so on, that I am not merely present in my body as a sailor is present in a ship, but that I am very closely joined and, as it were, intermingled with it, so that I and the body form a unit. If this were not so, I, who am nothing but a thinking thing, would not feel pain when the body was hurt, but would perceive the damage purely by the intellect, just as a sailor perceives by sight if anything in his ship is broken."

RENÉ DESCARTES

Remember, Unity begins with U.

"To be good is to be in harmony with oneself."

OSCAR WILDE

Self-awareness, honesty and self-respect are the first steps needed to create unity between heart, mind and body.

Be conscious of how you treat your mind, body and soul. When you notice moments of disharmony, pause, reflect, then forgive yourself and move on.

Five affirmations to chant for unity between mind, body and soul

1. I am worthy of respect and love.

2. I cherish and listen to my body.

3. I forgive myself for past mistakes.

4. I attract joy.

5. I am constantly growing.

Many of life's frustrations can be found where there is disunity between ambition and reality. Whether you're looking for a new job, trying to master a new skill or attempting to give up a bad habit, the trick isn't to accept dissatisfaction but to set realistic, achievable goals.

Four steps to unifying your dreams with reality

1. Set one concrete goal.

2. Take small steps to achieving your goal and work on it every day.

3. Monitor your efforts and reassess if necessary.

4. Keep going until you get there.

Three ways to create union between mind and body

1. When your mind tells you your body is tired: rest.

2. When your body tells you your mind is alert: move.

3. When your mind and body yearn for union: love.

"The reason why the world lacks unity, and lies broken and in heaps, is because man is disunited with himself."

RALPH WALDO EMERSON

Begin a unity log

1. Treat yourself to a lovely notebook. (Most of life's problems can be tackled with the assistance of gorgeous stationery.)

2. Start your unity log: identify the times in the day when there is disunity between your mind and body. For instance: your mind tells you to get up but your body is still exhausted.

3. By making yourself aware of when disunity arises, you can begin to usher in moments of unity.

4. Record in your Unity Log how you can transform moments of disunity into unity. Can you change your morning routine to allow a later alarm clock? Consider carefully each pinch point of disunity and think of practical solutions.

5. Reflect daily on the progress you are making from disunity to unity and, when harmony between mind and body is found, reward yourself with something that will satisfy both (shoes for example!).

Question: What is the result of unity between mind, body and spirit?

Answer: Health and happiness.

Unity...

Doesn't hold a grudge.

Embraces all.

Finds common ground.

Makes peace.

Celebrates together.

Invites all.

How to find the unity between your past, present and future

Are you still tripping up on an event from your past that is causing hurt in the present and affecting your future? Or are you hurtling towards the future, afraid to look backwards and ignoring your present life?

Finding unity throughout all periods of your life is a careful balancing act, but it is an important goal to strive for.

1. Give yourself time to contemplate your past

- Memory jars or journals are great ways of keeping positive moments from your past alive in the present. Consciously reflect on the past, but don't let it overwhelm you.

- Dust off and reframe photos of your family and ancestors and hang prominently in your home as reminders of what came before.

- Where past episodes are too painful to work through on your own, don't be afraid to seek professional help from a counsellor or therapist.

2. Give yourself time to live in the present

- Pay attention to what is good about your life now, today, this hour, this very minute. Write it down so you don't forget.

- Decide every morning to enjoy one pleasurable experience a day.

- Tell your loved ones just how much you love them.

3. Be mindful of your future

- Visualize what you would like to achieve this week, month or year.

- Don't wait for the perfect moment – get started!

- Have a back-up plan and stay flexible if things start to go awry.

Symbols of unity

Consider the rainbow as nature's way of showing diversity in unity. Though each colour can exist separately, they unite to create something of preternatural beauty.

The rainbow has also long been used to represent LGBT+ pride, with the united colours showing all the different shades of human sexuality and gender.

The circle is the perfect shape to symbolize unity. With no beginning or end, no direction or orientation, the circle is homogeneous, perfect and indivisible. A circle leads back to itself with all the points of the circumference equidistant from the centre.

It's no wonder circular rings are exchanged at wedding ceremonies to symbolize lifelong union and an unbreakable bond.

What better flower to represent unity than the allium? Bunches of alliums can grow from a single bulb, making this the perfect flower to represent togetherness.

In the language of flowers, alliums symbolize prosperity, patience and strength – all helpful qualities for a healthy relationship. Giving a bouquet of alliums is a sure way to create unity between flower giver and receiver.

Thinking about investing in some unity jewellery? Consider the infinity symbol, that elegant sideways figure of eight. Symbolizing eternity, the infinity sign is the perfect gift for a loved one; alternatively, buy one for yourself to represent your own connectedness with the universe.

Top 10 Unity anthems

'All For One', The Stone Roses

'Come Together', The Beatles

'El Mismo Sol (Under the Same Sun)', Alvaro Soler

'Join Together', The Who

'One Love', Bob Marley and the Wailers

'People are People', Depeche Mode

'Rainbowland', Miley Cyrus

'Strength in Numbers', Prophets of Rage

'United we Stand', Brotherhood of Man

'We are Family', Sister Sledge

American architect Donal McLaughlin designed the flag for the United Nations with a brief to capture world peace in graphic form – what a commission! On a blue background (blue being the opposite colour to the red of war) he created a graphic of a flattened earth embraced by olive branches. The result echoes the ancient wheel symbol – the oldest symbol of unity.

Alienation and loneliness can be symptoms of lack of unity in our lives. Sometimes we deliberately isolate from friends and family, and other times isolation is forced upon us. Restoring unity after a period of loneliness can be difficult, so be gentle with yourself as you take these small, daily steps towards unity.

How to reconnect with loved ones

1. Answer calls.

2. Make calls.

3. Reach out.

4. Let yourself be reached.

5. Give people the benefit of the doubt.

Three ways to foster unity in the community

1. Greet neighbours with a sincere smile.

2. Be hospitable and invite passing acquaintances for coffee to forge deeper connections.

3. Find common causes with those in your community.

The art of unity requires patience and a cool head. Next time a friend or family member expresses an opinion you disagree with, hold back on calling them out, stay quiet, wait. At a later date gently present your opinion as conversation, not conflict. That way, you will feel closer and more trusting and respectful of each other.

"Unity, agreement, is always silent or soft-voiced; it is only discord that loudly proclaims itself."

THOMAS CARLYLE

Remember: disagreement does not mean disunity. Unity accommodates different perspectives – it's about cohesion, not conformity.

From state banquets at Buckingham Palace to a kerbside kebab with a best friend, eating together is our most instinctive method of forging unity with others. Be generous with your hospitality: spread out the picnic rug, polish the cutlery, dust off the cookbooks and invite everyone over for a unity-inspired festival of food. After all, the more the merrier!

Three ways to host a unity feast

1. Invite friends and ask them all to bring their signature dish.

2. Organize a dinner crawl: have starters in one house, the main course next door, dessert on your friend's roof terrace and end with cheese and wine back at yours.

3. Cook double and share your meals with a household nearby.

Seven classic culinary unions

Fish & chips

Pizza & beer

Cheese & wine

Beef & horseradish

Bacon & eggs

Peanut butter & jelly

Mac & cheese

Culinary unions that should unscramble now... Discuss

Cheese & pineapple

Surf & turf

Bacon & maple syrup

Chocolate & chilli

Fries & mayo

When seeking togetherness, immerse yourself in spaces that model unity. In woodlands, for example, the whole circle of life can be appreciated. Listen to the birds and watch how they grub for insects. See how those insects thrive on the decaying leaf mould. Here, life and death are present before your eyes, continually enriching all the parts of nature and moving in complete harmony.

Visit your favourite woodland regularly to appreciate the unity of the seasons

Without the frost of winter there would be no heat of summer. Without the rain of spring the rich colours of autumn would not shine. Absorbing the ebb and flow of the seasons and the death and resurrection of woodland life teaches us that unity requires decay and rebirth; they unite to create the most wondrous of places.

"Let children walk with Nature, let them see the beautiful blendings and communions of death and life, their joyous inseparable unity, as taught in woods and meadows, plains and mountains and streams of our blessed star, and they will learn that death is stingless indeed, and as beautiful as life."

JOHN MUIR

Ecosystems are perfect examples of different beings working in harmony with each other, where the health of individual creatures is bound up with the health of the whole. Appreciating nature's ecosystems can nurture our own understanding that we too are part of a unified whole.

"*A life in harmony with nature, the love of truth and virtue, will purge the eyes to understand her text. By degrees we may come to know the primitive sense of the permanent objects of Nature, so that the world shall be to us an open book, and every form significant of the hidden life and final cause.*"

RALPH WALDO EMERSON

Volunteer to help maintain local green spaces

By helping to conserve areas of natural beauty, you'll be united with nature and local people, plus you'll make a huge difference to your local community.

Four best places to experience the unity of nature

1. Coral reefs.
2. Woodland.
3. Wildflower meadows.
4. A garden pond.

Blow the budget

1. Amazon Rainforest.
2. Great Barrier Reef.
3. Namib Desert.
4. Galapagos Islands.

Rituals for unity with nature

1. **Walk in the dew.** Greet nature skin-to-skin every morning by walking barefoot on the dew.

2. **Hug a tree.** Choose a big tall one that has stood many years on Earth. Place your arms around it and breathe in its history.

3. **Set up a wonder table.** Create an honoured space for the charms of nature you find. Cherish the acorn you find on a walk and bring home the jay's feather. When you feel disconnected from nature, you need only look to your collection.

"*What, then, is this unity of Nature?
Is it a fact or an imagination?
Is it a reality or a dream? Is it a
mere poetic fancy incapable of
definition; or is it a conception
firmly and legitimately founded
on the phenomena of the world?*"

DUKE OF ARGYLL

Create unity with Mother Nature by lending a helping hand

Help create unity between humankind and nature by reducing your impact on the Earth. Take simple steps to avoid excess waste:

1. Buy glass containers instead of plastic ones.

2. Shop local and give the plastic packaging a miss.

3. Next time your toothbrush needs replacing, invest in an electric one or, if you're on a tight budget, switch to bamboo.

Lessons in unity from the animal kingdom

1. **Combine your strengths.** To avoid predators, zebras and ostriches work together: the zebras bring their sharp eyesight while ostriches provide a keen sense of smell. Make like this pair and be better together.

2. **Hold on to your loved ones.** Otters hold hands while sleeping so they don't drift away from one another.

3. **Take it in turns.** When Canada geese fly in a V formation, they take turns being in the lead position to give each other a break.

Great unifiers of history: Abraham Lincoln

Abraham Lincoln's influence has reverberated down the ages and his example continues to inspire hope and goodness in the face of inequality.

The President of America from 1861 to 1865, Abraham Lincoln used his power to hold together an American Union that had been, as Lincoln said, 'conceived in liberty' and 'dedicated to the proposition that all men are created equal'.

Steering the Union to victory in the Civil War and issuing the Emancipation Proclamation whereby Congress prohibited slavery in all current and future United States, Abraham Lincoln did more than most figures in history to improve the lives of all people in society. His assassination was lamented by all who cherish notions of unity and the shared bonds of humanity.

Great unifiers of history:
Nelson Mandela

At the 1995 rugby world cup, Nelson Mandela committed an inspired act of unity that changed history forever by wearing the South African Springbok rugby jersey – a hated symbol of white supremacy in South Africa.

Mandela had spent 27 years imprisoned by the apartheid regime; that he should enter the Ellis Stadium as South Africa's President to a worldwide audience in such clothes was no insignificant gesture. By identifying with the largely white Afrikaner Springbok team, Mandela secured the roars of the predominantly white crowd who chanted his name over and over again.

His intention was to unite his country, the oppressors and the imprisoned, the rich and the poor, the white and black for a new, better future. President of South Africa from 1994 to 1999, Nelson Mandela was awarded the Nobel Peace Prize and is widely regarded as one of history's towering unifying figures.

Great unifiers of history: Desmond Tutu

As Chairman of the Truth and Reconciliation Commission (1996–2003), Archbishop Desmond Tutu achieved global acclaim for the Commission's attempts to heal the wrongs of apartheid in South Africa. In the unpicking of generations of savage racism and violence, Desmond Tutu sought not to judge and condemn but to listen and forgive. The attempt to forge a unified South Africa demanded that old wrongs were heard but vengeance was not sought. By keeping the unity of the future of the country at its heart, Desmond Tutu and the Commission were largely successful in easing the transition of South Africa to full democracy.

Desmond Tutu popularized the term 'Rainbow Nation' for South Africa and was awarded the Nobel Peace Prize in 1984 for his 'role as a unifying leader in the campaign to resolve the problem of apartheid in South Africa'.

> *"A house divided against itself cannot stand."*

ABRAHAM LINCOLN

The Latin phrase *Unus pro omnibus, omnes pro uno* translates to 'One for All, All for One' and is the unofficial motto of Switzerland.

The most famous historical example of the power of people to unite and form a country can be read in the text of the American Constitution, beginning with those powerful words, 'We the people'.

"We the People of the United States, in Order to form a more perfect Union, establish Justice, insure domestic Tranquility, provide for the common defence, promote the general Welfare, and secure the Blessings of Liberty to ourselves and our Posterity, do ordain and establish this Constitution for the United States of America."

*"By union the smallest states thrive.
By discord the greatest are destroyed."*

SALLUST

"Where there is unity, there is always victory."

PUBLILIUS SYRUS

Three united flags

1. **The United States flag.** The flag comprises 13 horizontal stripes – seven red alternating with six white stripes. The stripes represent the original 13 Colonies and the stars represent the 50 states of the Union. The red of the flag symbolizes hardiness and valour, white purity and innocence, and blue represents vigilance, perseverance and justice.

2. **The Union Jack.** This flag combines the crosses of the three countries which originally formed the United Kingdom: England (a red cross on a white background), Scotland (a diagonal white cross on a blue background) and Ireland (a diagonal red cross on a white background). The red cross for Ireland now only represents Northern Ireland.

3. **The Tricolour of France.** Following the violent upheavals of the French Revolution, the Tricolour was adopted in 1794, combining the revolutionary colours of red and blue used in Paris with Bourbon Royal white. The flag also symbolizes the French ideals of liberty, equality and fraternity.

Pub quiz question: How many countries contain the word United in their name?

Answer: 5

1. United Arab Emirates
2. United Kingdom of Great Britain and Northern Ireland
3. United Mexican States
4. United Republic of Tanzania
5. United States of America

"The point in history at which we stand is full of promise and of danger. The world will either move forward toward unity and widely shared prosperity or it will move apart."

FRANKLIN D. ROOSEVELT

Joe Biden, the 46th President of the United States, made an impassioned call for national unity in his inaugural speech on 20 January 2021. He emphasized the values of truth, democracy and unity in a hopeful vow to the people.

Even if it is not achieved, the pursuit of unity is still good in itself. American President Woodrow Wilson was tireless in his efforts to establish the League of Nations. In his famous Pueblo Speech in 1919, Wilson spoke in favour of America joining the League of Nations. Shortly afterwards he collapsed and suffered a massive stroke. Although the League of Nations did not prevent another world war, it did influence the formation of the United Nations.

> "*Friendship is the only cement that will ever hold the world together.*"

WOODROW WILSON

Most landmarks of liberty have been achieved by diverse groups of people uniting against tyranny and iniquity. Without unity there is no freedom.

- **1215 The Magna Carta** The barons unite against Bad King John.

- **1776 Declaration of Independence** The Colonists unite against the British.

- **1928 Women's voting rights** Suffragettes unite with MPs in favour of women's equal voting rights.

- **1944 D Day** Allies unite to defeat fascism.

- **1964 Civil Rights Act** All decent people unite against racial segregation.

"Even weak men when united are powerful."

FRIEDRICH SCHILLER

Jo Cox, a British Member of Parliament, made unity her defining political focus before she was tragically murdered in 2016. Her first speech in the House of Commons only a year before her death, in which she celebrated the benefits of immigration and diverse communities, became one of the most influential maiden speeches ever made.

"Remember, upon the conduct of each depends the fate of all."

ALEXANDER THE GREAT

The handshake is a free gesture that, especially in these post-lockdown times, can be revived to show common respect: two people literally reaching out to each other and creating a brief unified bond.

Famous unifying handshakes

In 1987, Princess Diana of Wales opened a dedicated HIV and AIDS unit at London Middlesex Hospital. She publicly shook hands with a patient with AIDS, helping to destigmatize the illness at the height of public fear around the virus. This one act helped promote kindness and unity in the face of fear.

In June 2012 HM The Queen shook hands with Martin McGuinness, Northern Ireland's former Deputy First Minister and former leader within the Provisional IRA. The historic act helped solidify peace between Northern Ireland and England.

Unity is thinking...

"Why not?"

"Let's try."

"We can work together."

"The more the merrier."

"Climb aboard."

Unity is perhaps not the most instinctive of emotions, for unity requires teamwork and the dimming of personal glory. The first step towards unity is humility. Understand that your family/work team/sports team/community will only succeed if individuals put the team before their own isolated fame.

Unity in adversity

Great upheavals, though terrible at the time, can bring together communities and unite them once the trauma has passed. The UK Office for National Statistics reported that from April to June 2020, more adults on average thought that Britain would be united after the country has recovered from the Coronavirus pandemic (46%) than thought the country was united before the pandemic (24%).

"Necessity unites hearts."

German proverb

Top Unity Hashtags

#WeStandTogether

#StrongerTogether

#UnitedWeStand

With their slogan 'All for one, and one for all!', Alexandre Dumas' heroes of *The Three Musketeers* perfectly exemplify the concept of unity in diversity. Despite the differences in their personalities and character – Porthos's strength of character (and eye for fashion), Athos's melancholy, and the lady-loving Aramis – they are nevertheless able to unite and fight for justice as one.

> *" The essence of the beautiful is unity in variety."*

FELIX MENDELSSOHN

" Find the good. Seek the Unity.
Ignore the divisions among us."

ARISTOTLE

Queen Latifah won a Grammy for her 1993 song U.N.I.T.Y., which addressed issues of female inequality. Not surprisingly for a song with such a powerful message, it remains Queen Latifah's biggest hit single in the US.

" *Truth in art is the unity of a thing with itself: the outward rendered expressive of the inward: the soul made incarnate: the body instinct with spirit. For this reason there is no truth comparable to sorrow.*"

OSCAR WILDE

Appreciating the power of unity allows us to recognize that alone we are unlikely to achieve much as a solitary being. Uniting with a person, tool, instrument or teacher allows our talents to develop and become more magnificent than we could ever have conceived alone.

What most creative duos have in common is an ability to complement the deficits of the other and unify to form something greater than the sum of their parts.

Begin learning a new skill – with a friend

Whether it's a musical instrument, a physical activity or picking up a new language, unity can be found in the mutual support you'll give to each other (and all the giggles you'll have when you make mistakes).

10 of the best partnerships

Asterix & Obelix

Astaire & Rogers

Batman & Robin

Ben & Jerry's

Bonnie & Clyde

Jeeves & Wooster

Mario & Luigi

Romeo & Juliet

Simon & Garfunkel

Tom & Jerry

What happens when Palestinian American scholar Edward Said and Israeli conductor and pianist Daniel Barenboim put aside cultural and religious differences and decide to create something magical with their shared love of music?

In 1999 they formed the West-Eastern Divan Orchestra, which brings together young musicians from Israel and the Arab countries. The musical enterprise promotes dialogue and unity of purpose between the various cultures of the Middle East and performs exquisite music across the globe. It is the epitome of the triumph of culture over conflict.

Ecumenicalism

When contemplating unity consider the Greek term *ecumenical* – the idea of 'the whole inhabited world'.

Ecumenicalism is currently used by Christians who belong to different denominations – Orthodox, Methodist, Baptist, Catholic – to work for closer unity.

The idea of ecumenicalism can also apply to non-religious life. From friendship groups to political movements, why get bogged down in small differences when there is an over-arching unity binding you together?

Unity requires humility and compassion. In order to achieve true harmony with others, learn to ditch the ego and think carefully about how you can support others.

Make the effort to meet people who are different to you, and forge connections with them

Instead of sticking to what you know, take the opportunity to learn from people with different experiences and backgrounds to you. The next time you're eating out for dinner, strike up a conversation with the waiter or waitress. Join an activity in unfamiliar parts of town. Listen more carefully to the people you already know and see what they can teach you.

'*Bhinneka Tunggal Ika*', the official motto of Indonesia, translates to 'In pieces, yet One' or 'Out of Unity, Diversity'. It hails from the Kakawin Sutasoma, a 14th-century Javanese poem that promotes unity between Buddhism and Hinduism.

> *"Divide and command, a wise maxim; Unite and guide, a better."*

JOHANN WOLFGANG VON GOETHE

Making eye contact builds trust and intimacy, and is even said to make you fall in love. The next time you have a disagreement with somebody close to you, look into each other's eyes for instant reconnection.

Look each other in the eyes

To overcome challenges and build unity within your relationship, take a few seconds to look deeply into each other's eyes. Hold your gaze for as long as you feel comfortable and feel yourselves reunite.

"In the long history of humankind (and animal kind, too) those who learned to collaborate and improvise most effectively have prevailed."

CHARLES DARWIN

When attempting to create unity with the people around you, be conscious of how you judge people and whether you are seeing the best in them. Often we judge others by their actions but ourselves by our intentions. In order to foster unity, be gracious enough to give others the benefit of the doubt and make allowances for others' faults.

Seeing the best in people is the first step in creating unity within your circle and community.

Unity means more than merely tolerating those people who are different to you. It means finding points of connection and joining them together like a jigsaw puzzle to make a greater whole.

Become an architect for unity

Seeking unity demands that when we encounter differences of opinion, of nationality, of religion, we build bridges, not walls. Be slow to judge and quick to believe in the goodness of the people around you.

Three ways to foster unity in an online workplace

1. Create virtual happy hours and coffee catch-ups to generate some office buzz.

2. Arrange virtual yoga sessions or exercise classes over lunch to foster a sense of physical togetherness.

3. Invite new staff to participate first to generate strong connections from the very beginning.

The golden rule for fostering unity in the workplace

Have a clear vision of your goal and how the individual strengths of your team members will help to achieve it. Valuing all contributions leads to better teamwork.

Whoever heard of a goalkeeper playing alone against a team of 11 footballers and winning? Or a violinist playing all the parts of an orchestra? Or an astronaut flying solo to the moon?

It is only in working in unity with others that humanity's greatest achievements are reached.

Join a sports team to feel the unity in action

What better way to feel the team spirit than by donning your sports shirt, putting in some serious effort and working in complete harmony with your team mates to play the best game possible?

The legend of King Arthur tells of his famous Round Table, with which he demonstrated true equality between his fellow knights; no one knight was to be given more importance than any other.

Be inspired by this trailblazer of 'roundtable discussions' and consider how your workplace unity could be improved with a sprinkling of early medieval corporate team bonding.

Fostering unity in the workplace – King Arthur style

- Be mindful of office furniture. If an actual round table is too unwieldy, could the furniture be rearranged in a more unity-inducing manner?

- The Knights of the Round Table were ruthlessly focussed on one task: the search for the Holy Grail. Having such a clear focus pays dividends for team cohesiveness.

- A series of hand-to-hand combats against errant knights or monsters might well be out of the question, but it's certainly worth booking a raft-building team bonding trip to build unity and turn colleagues into friends.

Unity does not mean that people need to be the same, but it does mean that they need to work together. True harmony requires hard work, a willingness to accept you are wrong and clear communication.

There is UNITY in COMM*UNITY* –
do what you can to keep it there.

Unity is open about saying. . .

"Never mind."

"Let's try again."

"I can help."

"Are you OK?"

"We can work it out."

"Please show me how."

Constantly arguing with your sister over the bathroom? Bickering with your partner over who should take out the trash? Stuck in a passive aggressive sticky note war with a housemate? It might be time to make a unity vow.

Consider which aspect of your relationship you seek to improve, then make a vow together.

Example of a unity vow

I promise myself and those around me I will seek unity when there is discord. When I cause pain, I will pause and strive for unity. When I feel sadness, I will remember the unity of those I love.

Think of great love or great friendship like a candy cane. Though they are two distinct parts, both spiral together in life to form a sweet united whole.

" Friendship is a union of spirits, a marriage of hearts, and the bond thereof virtue."

WILLIAM PENN

Follow the 3 Cs for family unity

1. **Commitment.** The foundation stone of all family relationships – a bid to commit to each other for a lifetime. Commit to looking out for your younger sister. Commit to supporting your parent as they change career. Commit to helping your aunt when she moves house. Work to maintain your family relationships and you will achieve greater familial harmony.

2. **Compassion.** No matter how irritating your family members might be, they are family and, first and foremost, they deserve compassion. Attempt to anger slowly and forgive easily.

3. **Communication.** This does not mean simply telling your family what you need, but also listening deeply to their concerns. Practise the art of sensitive conversations and your family unit will flourish.

Recipe for a united family

<u>Ingredients</u>

3 cups love

1 cup empathy

¼ cup patience

1 tbsp teamwork

<u>Method</u>

1. Blend together, adding more of each ingredient as needed.

2. Enjoy with an extra cup of love.

As a football team trains for victory, so must Team Family keep training regularly

1. Plan weekly Team Family evenings – films, dinner out, games night.

2. Engage in Team Family cheerleading – create a pinboard to celebrate each other's wins.

3. Honour Team Family traditions and forge new ones.

10 tips for a happy united family

1. Eat together around the table.

2. Read together.

3. Learn your family history.

4. Enjoy cross-generational events.

5. Stay in touch.

6. Contribute to the community as a family.

7. Consider multi-generational living.

8. Show an interest in each other.

9. Spend quality time together.

10. Ask each other regularly, 'How are you?'.

When creating more unity within a family, you must all agree on the goal of becoming more unified. To encourage intentional unity, pin a unity quote somewhere prominent in a communal area as a reminder of what you're working towards.

Three family unity mantras to live by

1. Our family is united by our love for each other.

2. Family unity gives us freedom to be ourselves.

3. We are better together.

" *There is no more sure tie between friends than when they are united in their objects and wishes.* **"**

MARCUS TULLIUS CICERO

"Three people gathering can create wisdom."

Japanese proverb

"Two heads are better than one."

English proverb

"When spider webs unite, they can tie up a lion."

Ethiopian proverb

"You cannot produce one human being without uniting two bodies."

Cameroonian proverb

Union rituals at weddings around the world

Tying the knot

Handfasting is the ancient Celtic tradition that gives us the phrase 'to tie the knot'. The bride and groom's hands are bound together with a cord or rope, which creates an infinity sign that is symbolic of a new union that will last forever.

Ceremony of the salt

This intimate Indian ritual, also known as 'datar', takes place in the groom's home and begins with the cleansing of the bride's feet. Then, droplets of milk are sprinkled in all corners of the house while the bride's head is covered. This is believed to help foster communication and avoid misunderstandings in the marriage.

After this, the bride and groom pass handfuls of salt to each other three times – without spilling any. This exchange is repeated with the groom's family. The intermingling of the salt represents the union of the couple.

'El lazo'

A tradition linked to Filipino, Mexican and Hispanic cultures, the 'lazo' refers to a lasso – usually a rosary, chain, rope or garland – which encircles the couple. The couple are unified to one another for life, and the lasso is kept as a symbol of this union.

The unity candle

An increasingly popular tradition that was first seen in American weddings in the 20th century, the lighting of the unity candle sees couples each light their own candle and then jointly enflame a unity candle between them.

Variations can include unity sand, water or wine, whereby participants pour the sand, water or wine from two separate containers into a beautiful glass jar.

The blanket ceremony

In some Native American cultures, a blanket ceremony is performed. First, the bride and groom are cloaked in separate blue blankets, which represent their past lives. Then, one white blanket is wrapped around both, symbolizing the union of the couple and their future life together.

" We try to realize the essential unity of the world with the conscious soul of man; we learn to perceive the unity held together by the one Eternal Spirit, whose power creates the earth, the sky, and the stars, and at the same time irradiates our minds with the light of a consciousness that moves and exists in unbroken continuity with the outer world."

RABINDRANATH TAGORE

I house within my heart the life
of things,
      All hearts athrob in the world I
felt as mine;
I shared the joy that in creation sings
      And drank its sorrow like a
poignant wine.

I have felt the anger in another's breast,
      All passions poured through my
world-self their waves;
One love I shared in a million bosoms
expressed.
      I am the beast man slays, the
beast he saves.

I spread life's burning wings of rapture and pain;
     Black fire and gold fire strove towards one bliss:
I rose by them towards a supernal plane
     Of power and love and deathless ecstasies.

A deep spiritual calm no touch can sway
Upholds the mystery of the Passion-play.

SRI AUROBINDO
'Life Unity'

The Japanese art of *kintsugi* – 'golden joinery' – is a 400-year-old practice which sees the repair of pottery with gold. The break is not hidden but highlighted and only adds to the history of the broken object, showing that by reuniting broken fragments something more beautiful and resilient can be created.

When a fight with a loved one leaves you hurting, take inspiration from the art of _kintsugi_

Instead of shying away from the situation, look for ways to reunite and grow from the experience. Do not be afraid of vulnerability; rather, be proud of your united strength.

Hollywood star Anne Hathaway is not only one of the world's most successful actresses but she's also dedicated to improving the lot of those less fortunate than herself. One of the many charities she supports is 'Friends Without A Border', a charity with a mission to provide compassionate medical care to children in Southeast Asia.

fwab.org

Lady Gaga's iconic album *Born This Way* so captured the hearts of young people that the singer established The Born This Way Foundation with her mother Cynthia Germanotta in 2012. Seeking to support the wellness of young people and working with them to make the world 'kinder and braver', the ethos of the foundation is very much centred on the notion of unity in all young people's glorious difference.

bornthisway.foundation

With her constant drum beat of togetherness, it is no surprise that Beyoncé is a supporter of the charity United Way. The charity fights for resources for communities across the globe, helping to provide access to education, healthcare and financial stability. By helping and uniting individuals, the work of United Way sees whole communities thrive.

unitedway.org

The beauty of unity lies in the idea that when all is said and done, we are one and the same. One of the unifying charities that Hollywood actor and singer Jennifer Hudson supports is Global Citizen. Their mission is to end poverty – with collective action and the power of unity.

globalcitizen.org

" *We all live with the objective of being happy; our lives are all different and yet the same.*"

ANNE FRANK

When there is unity, there is room for everyone.

QUOTES ARE TAKEN FROM

'Abdu'l-Bahá (1844–1921), leader of the Bahá'í Faith

Abraham Lincoln (1809–1865), 16th President of the United States

Aesop (c. 620 bc–564 bc), ancient Greek fabulist and storyteller

Alexander the Great (265–323 bc), ancient Greek King

Anne Frank (1929–1945), Jewish German-Dutch diarist who perished in Bergen-Belsen concentration camp

Aristotle (384–322 bc), Greek philosopher

Baal Shem Tov (1698–1760), Jewish Rabbi

Bahá'u'lláh (1817–1892), Persian religious leader

Charles Darwin (1809–1882), naturalist

Dogen (1200–1253), Japanese philosopher

Duke of Argyll (1823–1900), liberal politician and writer

Felix Mendelssohn (1809–1847), early Romantic German composer and pianist

Franklin Roosevelt (1882–1945), 32nd President of the United States

Friedrich Schiller (1759–1805), German playwright and polymath

Goethe (1749–1832), German polymath

Henry Melvill (1798–1871), English priest

Heraclitus (c. 535 BC–c. 475 BC), ancient Greek philosopher

John Locke (1632–1704), English philosopher

John Muir (1838–1914), advocate for the preservation of American wildernesses

Lao Tsu (571 BC–c. 5th-century BC), ancient Chinese founder of Taoism

Marcus Tullius Cicero (106 BC–43 BC), ancient Roman statesman and scholar

Oscar Wilde (1854–1900), English writer

Publilius Syrus (85–43 BC), Roman writer

Rabindranath Tagore (1861–1941), Indian poet

Ralph Waldo Emerson (1803–1882), American essayist

René Descartes (1596–1650), French philosopher and mathematician

Rumi (1207–1273), Persian poet

Sallust (86 BC–35 BC), Roman historian

Sri Aurobindo (1872–1950), Indian philosopher

Swami Vivekanada (1863–1902), Indian monk

Thomas Carlyle (1795–1881), Scottish historian

Thomas Paine (1737–1809), political philosopher

Thomas de Quincey (1785–1859), English essayist

Walt Whitman (1819–1892), American poet, journalist and essayist

William Penn (1644–1718), English writer and Quaker

Woodrow Wilson (1856–1924), 28th President of the United States

BIBLIOGRAPHY AND FURTHER READING

A–Z of Everything, Trevor Montague, Little Brown, 2001

History of Western Philosophy, Bertrand Russell, Routledge, 2004

The Oxford Dictionary of Quotations (5th ed), Oxford University Press, 2001

The Story of Philosophy, Bryan Magee, DK, 1998

USEFUL WEBSITES

archive.org

forbes.com

harvard.edu

psychologies.com

GET INVOLVED

fwab.org

bornthisway.foundation

unitedway.org

globalcitizen.org

amnestyusa.org

FIND YOUR LOCAL COMMUNITY

meetup.com

nextdoor.co.uk

gov.uk/find-a-community-support-group-or-organisation

Publishing Director Sarah Lavelle
Editorial Assistant Sofie Shearman
Words Joanna Gray
Series Designer Emily Lapworth
Designer Alicia House
Head of Production Stephen Lang
Production Controller Sabeena Atchia

Published in 2022 by Quadrille,
an imprint of Hardie Grant
Publishing

Quadrille
52–54 Southwark Street
London SE1 1UN
quadrille.com

The publisher has made every
effort to trace the copyright
holders. We apologize in advance
for any unintentional omissions
and would be pleased to insert the
appropriate acknowledgement in
any subsequent edition.

Cataloguing in Publication Data:
a catalogue record for this book is
available from the British Library.

ISBN 978 1 78713 800 1

Printed in China